To

_____

From

_____

Date

_____

Freeman-Smith, a division of Worthy Media, Inc.

134 Franklin Road, Suite 200, Brentwood, Tennessee 37027

The quoted ideas expressed in this book (but not Scripture verses) are not, in all cases, exact quotations, as some have been edited for clarity and brevity. In all cases, the author has attempted to maintain the speaker's original intent. In some cases, quoted material for this book was obtained from secondary sources, primarily print media. While every effort was made to ensure the accuracy of these sources, the accuracy cannot be guaranteed. For additions, deletions, corrections, or clarifications in future editions of this text, please write Freeman-Smith.

Scripture quotations are taken from:

The Holy Bible, King James Version

The Holy Bible, New International Version (NIV) Copyright © 1973, 1978, 1984, by International Bible Society. Used by permission of Zondervan Publishing House. All rights reserved.

The Holy Bible, New King James Version (NKJV) Copyright © 1982 by Thomas Nelson, Inc. Used by permission.

The New American Standard Bible®, (NASB) Copyright © 1960, 1962, 1963, 1968, 1971, 1972, 1973, 1975, 1977, 1995 by The Lockman Foundation. Used by permission.

Holy Bible, New Living Translation, (NLT) Copyright © 1996. Used by permission of Tyndale House Publishers, Inc., Wheaton, Illinois 60189. All rights reserved.

The Message (MSG)- This edition issued by contractual arrangement with NavPress, a division of The Navigators, U.S.A. Originally published by NavPress in English as THE MESSAGE: The Bible in Contemporary Language copyright 2002-2003 by Eugene Peterson. All rights reserved.

New Century Version®. (NCV) Copyright © 1987, 1988, 1991 by Word Publishing, a division of Thomas Nelson, Inc. All rights reserved. Used by permission.

The Holman Christian Standard Bible™ (HCSB) Copyright © 1999, 2000, 2001 by Holman Bible Publishers. Used by permission.

Cover Design by Scott Williams/ Richmond & Williams
Page Layout by Bart Dawson

ISBN 978-1-60587-456-2

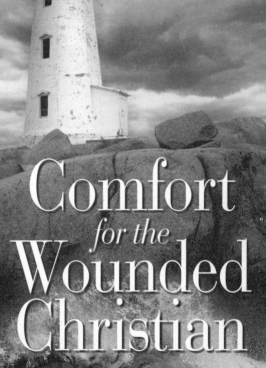

Comfort
for the
Wounded
Christian

Introduction

We know that all things work together for the good of those who love God: those who are called according to His purpose.

Romans 8:28 HCSB

God's Word promises that all things work together for the good of those who love Him. Yet sometimes we encounter situations that seem so troubling—or so tragic—that we simply cannot comprehend how these events might be a part of God's plan for our lives. We experience some deeply significant loss: perhaps the death of a loved one; perhaps the loss of health; perhaps divorce, job loss, or a broken personal relationship. Whatever the nature of the loss, its pain is so profound that we honestly wonder if recovery is possible. But with God, all things are possible.

The Christian faith, as communicated through the words of the Holy Bible, is a healing faith. It offers comfort in times of trouble, courage for our fears, hope instead of hopelessness. For Christians, the grave is not a final resting place; it is a place of transition. Through the healing words of God's promises, Christians understand that the Lord continues to manifest His plan in good times and bad.

If you are experiencing the intense pain of a recent loss, or if you are still mourning a loss from

long ago, this book is intended to remind you that
God is always reaching out to comfort you and to
heal you. Your job, simply put, is to let Him.

Day 1

God's Plan and Your Tough Times

Who are those who fear the Lord? He will show them the path they should choose. They will live in prosperity, and their children will inherit the Promised Land.

Psalm 25:12-13 NLT

It's an age-old riddle: Why does God allow us to suffer? After all, since we trust that God is all-powerful, and since we trust that His hand shapes our lives, why doesn't He simply rescue us—and our loved ones—from all hardship and pain?

God's Word teaches us again and again that He loves us and wants the best for us. And the Bible also teaches us that God is ever-present and always watchful. So why, we wonder, if God is really so concerned with every detail of our lives, does He permit us to endure emotions like grief, sadness, shame, or fear? And why does He allow tragic circumstances to invade the lives of good people? These questions perplex us, especially when times are tough.

On occasion, all of us face adversity, and throughout life, we all must endure life-changing personal losses that leave us breathless. When we pass through the dark valleys of life, we often ask, "Why me?" Sometimes, of course, the answer is ob-

7

vious—sometimes we make mistakes, and we must pay for them. But on other occasions, when we have done nothing wrong, we wonder why God allows us to suffer.

Even when we cannot understand God's plans, we must trust them. And even when we are impatient for our situations to improve, we must trust God's timing. If we seek to live in accordance with His plan for our lives, we must continue to study His Word (in good times and bad), and we must be watchful for His signs, knowing that in time, He will lead us through the valleys, onward to the mountaintop.

So, if you've been wounded by tough times, don't give up and don't give in. God still has glorious plans for you. So keep your eyes and ears open . . . as well as your heart.

Every misfortune, every failure,
every loss may be transformed.
God has the power to transform
all misfortunes into "God-sends."

—

Mrs. Charles E. Cowman

More From God's Word About God's Plan

"For I know the plans I have for you," declares the Lord, "plans to prosper you and not to harm you, plans to give you hope and a future. Then you will call upon me and come and pray to me, and I will listen to you."

Jeremiah 29:11-12 NIV

And we know that in all things God works for the good of those who love him, who have been called according to his purpose.

Romans 8:28 NIV

He replied, "Every plant that My heavenly Father didn't plant will be uprooted."

Matthew 15:13 HCSB

The steps of the Godly are directed by the Lord. He delights in every detail of their lives. Though they stumble, they will not fall, for the Lord holds them by the hand.

Psalm 37:23-24 NLT

It is God who works in you to will and to act according to his good purpose.

Philippians 2:13 NIV

More Powerful Ideas About God's Plan

Each problem is a God-appointed instructor.

Charles Swindoll

Our loving God uses difficulty in our lives to burn away the sin of self and build faith and spiritual power.

Bill Bright

On the darkest day of your life, God is still in charge. Take comfort in that.

Marie T. Freeman

When terrible things happen, there are two choices, and only two: We can trust God, or we can defy Him. We believe that God is God, He's still got the whole world in His hands and knows exactly what He's doing, or we must believe that He is not God and that we are at the awful mercy of mere chance.

Elisabeth Elliot

Don't let circumstances distress you. Rather, look for the will of God for your life to be revealed in and through those circumstances.

Billy Graham

Day 2

It's Possible to Heal

Is anything too hard for the LORD?

Genesis 18:14 KJV

When you experience the emotional pain of a significant loss, you may wonder if you'll ever recover. When the feelings of sorrow are intense, you may think—mistakenly—that the suffering will never subside. But the good news is this: while time heals many wounds, God has the power to heal them all.

Ours is a God of infinite power and infinite possibilities. But sometimes, because of limited faith and limited understanding, we wrongly assume that God cannot or will not intervene in the affairs of everyday life. Such assumptions are simply wrong.

God is busily at work in the world, and your world. Your job is to ask Him—fervently and often—for the things you need.

Have you sincerely asked God for His help as you begin the healing process? Have you asked Him to lead you on the first step back to recovery? Have you prayed for the peace that passes all understanding? If so, you're on the right track. If not, it's time to abandon your doubts and reclaim your faith in God's promises.

God's Holy Word makes it clear: absolutely nothing is impossible for Him. And since the Bible means what it says, you can be comforted in the knowledge that the Creator of the universe can do miraculous things in your own life and in the lives of your loved ones. Your challenge, as a believer, is to take God at His word, and to wait patiently for Him to comfort you with the peace that flows from His miraculous healing touch.

The grace of God is sufficient for
all our needs, for every problem and for
every difficulty, for every broken heart,
and for every human sorrow.

—

Peter Marshall

More From God's Word About God's Power

For His divine power has given us everything required for life and godliness, through the knowledge of Him who called us by His own glory and goodness.

2 Peter 1:3 HCSB

For the LORD your God is God of gods and Lord of lords, the great God, mighty and awesome.

Deuteronomy 10:17 NIV

I pray also that you will have greater understanding in your heart so you will know the hope to which he has called us and that you will know how rich and glorious are the blessings God has promised his holy people. And you will know that God's power is very great for us who believe.

Ephesians 1:18-19 NCV

With God's power working in us, God can do much, much more than anything we can ask or imagine.

Ephesians 3:20 NCV

Proclaim the power of God, whose majesty is over Israel, whose power is in the skies. You are awesome, O God, in your sanctuary; the God of Israel gives power and strength to his people. Praise be to God!

Psalm 68:34-35 NIV

More Powerful Ideas About God's Power

God can heal the brokenhearted if all the pieces are given to Him.

Warren Wiersbe

When we face an impossible situation, all self-reliance and self-confidence must melt away; we must be totally dependent on Him for the resources.

Anne Graham Lotz

I believe that the Creator of this universe takes delight in turning the terrors and tragedies that come with living in this old, fallen domain of the devil and transforming them into something that strengthens our hope, tests our faith, and shows forth His glory.

Al Green

Whatever hallway you're in—no matter how long, how dark, or how scary—God is right there with you.

Bill Hybels

As sure as God puts his children in the furnace, he will be in the furnace with them.

C. H. Spurgeon

Day 3

Where to Take Your Worries

Don't worry about anything, but in everything, through prayer and petition with thanksgiving, let your requests be made known to God.

Philippians 4:6 HCSB

Because we have the ability to think, we also have the ability to worry. All of us, even the most faithful believers, are plagued by occasional periods of discouragement and doubt. Even though we hold tightly to God's promise of salvation—even though we sincerely believe in God's love and protection—we may find ourselves fretting over the countless details of everyday life.

Because of His humanity, Jesus understood the inevitability of worry. And He addressed the topic clearly and forcefully in the 6th chapter of Matthew:

Therefore I say to you, do not worry about your life, what you will eat or what you will drink; nor about your body, what you will put on. Is not life more than food and the body more than clothing? Look at the birds of the air, for they neither sow nor reap nor gather into barns; yet your heavenly Father feeds them. Are you not of more value than they? Which of you by worrying

can add one cubit to his stature? . . . Therefore do not
worry about tomorrow, for tomorrow will worry about
its own things. Sufficient for the day is its own trouble.
(vv. 25-27, 34 NKJV)

More often than not, our worries stem from an
inability to focus and to trust. We fail to focus on
a priceless gift from God: the profound, precious,
present moment. Instead of thanking God for the
blessings of this day, we choose to fret about two
more ominous days: yesterday and tomorrow. We
stew about the unfairness of the past, or we agonize
about the uncertainty of the future. Such thinking
stirs up negative feelings that prepare our hearts and
minds for an equally destructive emotion: fear.

Our fears are rooted in a failure to trust. Instead of trusting God's plans for our lives, we fix
our minds on countless troubles that might come
to pass (but seldom do). A better strategy, of course,
is to take God at His word by trusting His promises. Our Lord has promised that He will care for our
needs—needs, by the way, that He understands far
more completely than we do. God's Word is unam-
biguous; so, too, should our trust be in Him.

In Matthew 6, Jesus instructs us to live in day-
tight compartments. He reminds us that each day
has enough worries of its own without the added
weight of yesterday's regrets or tomorrow's fears.
Perhaps you feel disturbed by the past or threatened
by the future. Perhaps you are concerned about

your relationships, your health, or your finances. Or perhaps you are simply a "worrier" by nature. If so, make Matthew 6 a regular part of your daily Bible reading. This beautiful passage will remind you that God still sits in His heaven and you are His beloved child. Then, perhaps, you will worry less and trust God more. And that's as it should be because God is trustworthy . . . and you are protected.

Never yield to gloomy anticipation.
Place your hope and confidence in God.
He has no record of failure.

—

Mrs. Charles E. Cowman

More From God's Word About
Overcoming Anxiety

I will be with you when you pass through the waters . . . when you walk through the fire . . . the flame will not burn you. For I the Lord your God, the Holy One of Israel, and your Savior.

Isaiah 43:2-3 HCSB

Your heart must not be troubled. Believe in God; believe also in Me.

John 14:1 HCSB

Come to Me, all you who labor and are heavy laden, and I will give you rest. Take My yoke upon you and learn from Me, for I am gentle and lowly in heart, and you will find rest for your souls. For My yoke is easy and My burden is light.

Matthew 11:28-30 NKJV

Those who trust in the Lord are like Mount Zion. It cannot be shaken; it remains forever.

Psalm 125:1 HCSB

Be strong and courageous, and do the work. Don't be afraid or discouraged, for the Lord God, my God, is with you. He won't leave you or forsake you.

1 Chronicles 28:20 HCSB

More Powerful Ideas About Worry

Worry is the senseless process of cluttering up to-morrow's opportunities with leftover problems from today.

Barbara Johnson

Pray, and let God worry.

Martin Luther

Today is mine. Tomorrow is none of my business. If I peer anxiously into the fog of the future, I will strain my spiritual eyes so that I will not see clearly what is required of me now.

Elisabeth Elliott

Worry and anxiety are sand in the machinery of life; faith is the oil.

E. Stanley Jones

Anxiety may be natural and normal for the world, but it is not to be part of a believer's lifestyle.

Kay Arthur

Day 4

Making Peace with Your Past

Do not remember the past events, pay no attention to things of old. Look, I am about to do something new; even now it is coming. Do you not see it? Indeed, I will make a way in the wilderness, rivers in the desert.

Isaiah 43:18-19 HCSB

The American theologian Reinhold Niebuhr composed a profoundly simple verse that came to be known as the Serenity Prayer: "God, grant me the serenity to accept the things I cannot change, the courage to change the things I can, and the wisdom to know the difference." Niebuhr's words are far easier to recite than they are to live by. Why? Because most of us want life to unfold in accordance with our own wishes and timetables. But sometimes God has other plans.

One of the things that fits nicely into the category of "things we cannot change" is the past. Yet even though we know that the past is unchangeable, many of us continue to invest energy worrying about the unfairness of yesterday (when we should, instead, be focusing on the opportunities of today and the promises of tomorrow). Author Hannah Whitall Smith observed, "How changed our lives would be if we could only fly through the days on wings of surrender and trust!" These words remind us that even when we cannot understand the past, we must trust God and accept His will.

So, if you've endured a difficult past, accept it and learn from it, but don't spend too much time here in the precious present fretting over memories of the unchangeable past. Instead, trust God's plan and look to the future. After all, the future is where everything that's going to happen to you from this moment on is going to take place.

The pages of your past cannot be rewritten, but the pages of your tomorrows are blank.

—

Zig Ziglar

More From God's Word About
Accepting the Past

All bitterness, anger and wrath, insult and slander must be removed from you, along with all wickedness. And be kind and compassionate to one another, forgiving one another, just as God also forgave you in Christ.

Ephesians 4:31-32 HCSB

Should we accept only good from God and not adversity?

Job 2:10 HCSB

I have learned, in whatsoever state I am, therewith to be content.

Philippians 4:11 KJV

Brothers, I do not consider myself to have taken hold of it. But one thing I do: forgetting what is behind and reaching forward to what is ahead, I pursue as my goal the prize promised by God's heavenly call in Christ Jesus.

Philippians 3:13-14 HCSB

For if you forgive people their wrongdoing, your heavenly Father will forgive you as well. But if you don't forgive people, your Father will not forgive your wrongdoing.

Matthew 6:14-15 HCSB

More Powerful Ideas About
Accepting the Past

Our yesterdays teach us how to savor our todays and tomorrows.

Patsy Clairmont

The devil keeps so many of us stuck in our weakness. He reminds us of our pasts when we ought to remind him of his future—he doesn't have one.

Franklin Graham

If you are God's child, you are no longer bound to your past or to what you were. You are a brand new creature in Christ Jesus.

Kay Arthur

We need to be at peace with our past, content with our present, and sure about our future, knowing they are all in God's hands.

Joyce Meyer

Leave the broken, irreversible past in God's hands, and step out into the invincible future with Him.

Oswald Chambers

The Grieving Process

The Lord is near to those who have a broken heart.

Psalm 34:18 NKJV

Grief is a uniquely personal experience. But grief is also a universal experience, a journey that has been clearly mapped by those who have documented the common elements of human suffering.

Grief usually begins with shock and then gives way to intense pain. Over time, as the mourner regains his or her emotional balance, the pain begins to fade. Gradually—sometimes almost imperceptibly—a new life is raised from the ashes of the old. And even though the mourner may never "get over" his losses, he can, in time, reorganize his life and move beyond the intensity of the initial pain. Some losses are, of course, so profound and so painful that a mourner is forever changed. But for Christians who place their faith completely in their Creator—and in His only begotten Son—the experience of grief is different in one very important respect: Christians face grief armed with God's promises.

Through the Holy Bible, God promises to comfort and heal those who call upon Him. And He promises that the grave is not a final resting place;

it is, instead, merely a place of transition—a weigh station on the path to eternal life—for those who give their hearts to God's Son.

As you ponder the ideas contained in this book, think carefully about your own situation: your emotions, your thoughts, your experiences, and your pain. And as you do, think carefully about the ways that you're responding to your own particular losses. The more you understand about the grieving process—and the more you understand about your own grieving process—the better you can cope with its many twists and turns. But whatever the nature of your loss, always remember this overriding truth: God is with you, God is good, and you are protected.

Grief is the aftermath of
any deeply significant loss.

—

Wayne Oates

More From God's Word About Grief

God will wipe away every tear from their eyes.

Revelation 7:17 HCSB

Weeping may go on all night, but joy comes with the morning.

Psalm 30:5 NLT

When I sit in darkness, the Lord will be a light to me.

Micah 7:8 NKJV

Blessed are those who mourn, for they will be comforted.

Matthew 5:4 NIV

So you also have sorrow now. But I will see you again. Your hearts will rejoice, and no one will rob you of your joy.

John 16:22 HCSB

More Powerful Ideas About Grief

God's Word never said we were not to grieve our losses. It says we are not to grieve as those who have no hope (1 Thessalonians 4:13). Big difference.

Beth Moore

There is no pit so deep that God's love is not deeper still.

Corrie ten Boom

The kingdom of God is a kingdom of paradox, where through the ugly defeat of a cross, a holy God is utterly glorified. Victory comes through defeat; healing through brokenness; finding self through losing self.

Chuck Colson

Suffering is no argument of God's displeasure; it is simply a part of the fiber of our lives.

Fanny Crosby

When the full impact of our loss hit home, it seemed that everything moved in slow motion.

Zig Ziglar

Day 6

Beyond Fear

Indeed, God is my salvation. I will trust [Him] and not be afraid.

Isaiah 12:2 HCSB

All of us may find our courage tested by the inevitable disappointments and tragedies of life. After all, ours is a world filled with uncertainty, hardship, sickness, and danger. Old Man Trouble, it seems, is never too far from the front door.

When we focus upon our fears and our doubts, we may find many reasons to lie awake at night and fret about the uncertainties of the coming day. A better strategy, of course, is to focus not upon our fears, but instead upon our God.

God is as near as your next breath, and He is in control. He offers salvation to all His children, including you. God is your shield and your strength; you are His forever. So don't focus your thoughts upon the fears of the day. Instead, trust God's plan and His eternal love for you. And remember: God is good, and He has the last word.

God Can Handle It

It's a promise that is made over and over again in the Bible: Whatever "it" is, God can handle it.

Life isn't always easy. Far from it! Sometimes, life can be very, very tough. But even then, even during our darkest moments, we're protected by a loving Heavenly Father. When we're worried, God can reassure us; when we're sad, God can comfort us. When our hearts are broken, God is not just near; He is here. So we must lift our thoughts and prayers to Him. When we do, He will answer our prayers. Why? Because He is our shepherd, and He has promised to protect us now and forever.

Fear is a self-imposed prison that
will keep you from becoming
what God intends for you to be.

Rick Warren

More From God's Word About
Overcoming Fear

Even when I go through the darkest valley, I fear [no] danger, for You are with me.

Psalm 23:4 HCSB

Don't be afraid. Only believe.

Mark 5:36 HCSB

For I, the Lord your God, hold your right hand and say to you: Do not fear, I will help you.

Isaiah 41:13 HCSB

I sought the Lord, and He heard me, and delivered me from all my fears.

Psalm 34:4 NKJV

Do not fear, for I am with you; do not be afraid, for I am your God. I will strengthen you; I will help you; I will hold on to you with My righteous right hand.

Isaiah 41:10 HCSB

More Powerful Ideas About
Overcoming Fear

When we meditate on God and remember the promises He has given us in His Word, our faith grows, and our fears dissolve.

Charles Stanley

The Bible is a Christian's guidebook, and I believe the knowledge it sheds on pain and suffering is the great antidote to fear for suffering people. Knowledge can dissolve fear as light destroys darkness.

Philip Yancey

God shields us from most of the things we fear, but when He chooses not to shield us, He unfailingly allots grace in the measure needed.

Elisabeth Elliot

Only believe, don't fear. Our Master, Jesus, always watches over us, and no matter what the persecution, Jesus will surely overcome it.

Lottie Moon

If we do not tremble before God, the world's system seems wonderful to us and pleasantly consumes us.

James Montgomery Boice

Understanding Depression

Weeping may go on all night, but joy comes with the morning.

Psalm 30:5 NLT

Throughout our lives, all of us must endure personal losses that leave us struggling to find hope. The sadness that accompanies such losses is an inescapable fact of life—but in time, we move beyond our grief as the sadness runs its course and life returns to normal. Depression, however, is more than sadness.

Depression is a physical and emotional condition that is, in almost all cases, treatable with medication and counseling. And it is not a disease to be taken lightly. Left untreated, depression presents real dangers to patients' physical health and to their emotional well-being.

If you're feeling blue, perhaps it's a logical response to the disappointments of everyday life. But if your feelings of sadness have lasted longer than you think they should—or if someone close to you fears that your sadness may have evolved into clinical depression—it's time to seek professional help.

Here are a few simple guidelines to consider as you make decisions about possible treatment:

1. If your feelings of sadness have resulted in persistent and prolonged changes in sleep patterns, or if you've experienced a significant change in weight (either gain or loss), consult your physician. 2. If you have persistent urges toward self-destructive behavior, or if you feel as though you have lost the will to live, consult a professional counselor or physician immediately. 3. If someone you trust urges you to seek counseling, schedule a session with a professionally trained counselor to evaluate your condition. 4. If you are plagued by consistent, prolonged, severe feelings of hopelessness, consult a physician, a professional counselor, or your pastor.

God's Word has much to say about every aspect of your life, including your emotional health. And, when you face concerns of any sort—including symptoms of depression—remember that God is with you. Your Creator Father intends that His joy should become your joy. Yet sometimes, amid the inevitable hustle and bustle of life, you may forfeit—albeit temporarily—God's joy as you wrestle with the challenges of daily living.

So, if you're feeling genuinely depressed, trust your medical doctor to do his or her part. Then, place your ultimate trust in your benevolent Heavenly Father. His healing touch, like His love, endures forever.

More From God's Word About
God's Support

Now the God of all grace, who called you to His eternal glory in Christ Jesus, will personally restore, establish, strengthen, and support you.

1 Peter 5:10 HCSB

The LORD is my strength and song, and He has become my salvation; He is my God, and I will praise Him...

Exodus 15:2 NKJV

Peace, peace to you, and peace to your helpers! For your God helps you.

1 Chronicles 12:18 NKJV

He gives power to the weak, and to those who have no might He increases strength.

Isaiah 40:29 NKJV

I am able to do all things through Him who strengthens me.

Philippians 4:13 HCSB

More Powerful Ideas About
Negative Emotions

Feelings of uselessness and hopelessness are not from God, but from the evil one, the devil, who wants to discourage you and thwart your effectiveness for the Lord.

Bill Bright

What the devil loves is that vague cloud of unspecified guilt feeling or unspecified virtue by which he lures us into despair or presumption.

C. S. Lewis

In the soul-searching of our lives, we are to stay quiet so we can hear Him say all that He wants to say to us in our hearts.

Charles Swindoll

I am sure it is never sadness—a proper, straight, natural response to loss—that does people harm, but all the other things, all the resentment, dismay, doubt and self-pity with which it is usually complicated.

C. S. Lewis

Emotions we have not poured out in the safe hands of God can turn into feelings of hopelessness and depression. God is safe.

Beth Moore

35

Day 8

Renewed and Comforted
Day by Day

Every morning he wakes me. He teaches me to listen
like a student. The Lord God helps me learn...

Isaiah 50:4-5 NCV

Each new day is a gift from God, and if you are wise,
you will spend a few quiet moments each morning
thanking the Giver. When you do, you'll discover
that time spent with God can lift your spirits and
relieve your stress.

Warren Wiersbe writes, "Surrender your mind
to the Lord at the beginning of each day." And that's
sound advice. When you begin each day with your
head bowed and your heart lifted, you are reminded
of God's love, His protection, and His commandments. Then, you can align your priorities for the
coming day with the teachings and commandments
that God has placed upon your heart.

So, if you've acquired the unfortunate habit of
trying to "squeeze" God into the corners of your life,
it's time to reshuffle the items on your to-do list by
placing God first. And if you haven't already done
so, form the habit of spending quality time with
your Father in heaven. He deserves it . . . and so
do you.

Pray About It

Andrew Murray observed, "Some people pray just to pray, and some people pray to know God." Your task, as a maturing believer, is to pray, not out of habit or obligation, but out of a sincere desire to know your Heavenly Father. Through constant prayers, you should petition God, you should praise Him, and you should seek to discover His unfolding plans for your life.

Today, reach out to the Giver of all blessings. Turn to Him for guidance and for strength. Invite Him into every corner of your day. Ask Him to teach you and to lead you. And remember that no matter your circumstances, God is never far away; He is here . . . always right here. So pray.

The moment you wake up each morning, all your wishes and hopes for the day rush at you like wild animals. And the first job each morning consists in shoving it all back; in listening to that other voice, taking that other point of view, letting that other, larger, stronger, quieter life coming flowing in.

—

C. S. Lewis

More From God's Word About Worshipping God Every Day

Teach me Your way, Lord, and I will live by Your truth. Give me an undivided mind to fear Your name.

Psalm 86:11 HCSB

I will instruct you and show you the way to go; with My eye on you, I will give counsel.

Psalm 32:8 HCSB

Happy is the man who finds wisdom, and the man who gains understanding.

Proverbs 3:13 NKJV

But grow in the grace and knowledge of our Lord and Savior Jesus Christ. To Him be the glory both now and to the day of eternity.

2 Peter 3:18 HCSB

In all your ways acknowledge Him, and He shall direct your paths.

Proverbs 3:6 NKJV

More Powerful Ideas About
Your Daily Devotional

Every morning God gives us the gift of comprehending anew His faithfulness of old; thus in the midst of our life with God, we may daily begin a new life with Him.

Dietrich Bonhoeffer

Think of this—we may live together with Him here and now, a daily walking with Him who loved us and gave Himself for us.

Elisabeth Elliot

I suggest you discipline yourself to spend time daily in a systematic reading of God's Word. Make this "quiet time" a priority that nobody can change.

Warren Wiersbe

Jesus challenges you and me to keep our focus daily on the cross of His will if we want to be His disciples.

Anne Graham Lotz

I think that God required the Israelites to gather manna every morning so that they would learn to come to Him daily.

Cynthia Heald

Day 9

The Right Kind of Attitude

For God has not given us a spirit of fearfulness, but one of power, love, and sound judgment.

2 Timothy 1:7 HCSB

If you want to build a better future for yourself and your family, you need the right kind of attitude: the positive kind. So what's your attitude today? Are you fearful, angry, bored, or worried? Are you pessimistic, perplexed, pained, and perturbed? Are you moping around with a frown on your face that's almost as big as the one in your heart? If so, God wants to have a little talk with you.

God created you in His own image, and He wants you to experience joy, contentment, peace, and abundance. But, God will not force you to experience these things; you must claim them for yourself.

God has given you free will, including the ability to influence the direction and the tone of your thoughts. And, here's how God wants you to direct those thoughts:

"Finally brothers, whatever is true, whatever is honorable, whatever is just, whatever is pure, whatever is lovely, whatever is commendable—if there is any

moral excellence and if there is any praise—dwell on these things" (Philippians 4:8 HCSB).

The quality of your attitude will help determine the quality of your life, so you must guard your thoughts accordingly. If you make up your mind to approach life with a healthy mixture of realism and optimism, you'll be rewarded. But, if you allow yourself to fall into the unfortunate habit of negative thinking, you will doom yourself to unhappiness, or mediocrity, or worse.

So, the next time you find yourself dwelling upon the negative aspects of your life, refocus your attention on things positive. The next time you find yourself falling prey to the blight of pessimism, stop yourself and turn your thoughts around. The next time you're tempted to waste valuable time gossiping or complaining, resist those temptations with all your might.

And remember: You'll never whine your way to the top . . . so don't waste your breath.

Follow His Lead

God promises that He has the power to transform your life if you invite Him to do so. Your decision, then, is straightforward: whether or not to allow the Father's transforming power to work in you and through you.

God stands at the door of your heart and waits; all you must do is to invite Him in. When you do so, you cannot remain unchanged.

Is there some aspect of your life you'd like to change—a bad habit, an unhealthy relationship, or a missed opportunity? Then ask God to change your attitude and guide your path. Talk specifically to your Creator about the person you are today and the person you want to become tomorrow. When you sincerely petition the Father, you'll be amazed at the things that He and you, working together, can accomplish.

Attitude is more important than the past, than education, than money, than circumstances, than what people do or say. It is more important than appearance, giftedness, or skill.

—

Charles Swindoll

More From God's Word About Your Attitude

Set your mind on things above, not on things on the earth.

Colossians 3:2 NKJV

Come near to God, and God will come near to you. You sinners, clean sin out of your lives. You who are trying to follow God and the world at the same time, make your thinking pure.

James 4:8 NCV

Those who are pure in their thinking are happy, because they will be with God.

Matthew 5:8 NCV

In everything give thanks; for this is the will of God in Christ Jesus for you.

1 Thessalonians 5:18 NKJV

Worship the Lord with gladness. Come before him, singing with joy. Acknowledge that the Lord is God! He made us, and we are his. We are his people, the sheep of his pasture.

Psalm 100:2-3 NLT

More Powerful Ideas About
The Importance of a Positive Attitude

We are either the masters or the victims of our attitudes. It is a matter of personal choice. Who we are today is the result of choices we made yesterday. Tomorrow, we will become what we choose today. To change means to choose to change.

John Maxwell

The mind is like a clock that is constantly running down. It has to be wound up daily with good thoughts.

Fulton J. Sheen

The difference between winning and losing is how we choose to react to disappointment.

Barbara Johnson

It's your choice: you can either count your blessings or recount your disappointments.

Jim Gallery

Pain is inevitable, but misery is optional.

Max Lucado

Day 10

Don't Give Up!

No matter how many times you trip them up, God-loyal people don't stay down long; Soon they're up on their feet, while the wicked end up flat on their faces.

Proverbs 24:16 MSG

The old saying is as true today as it was when it was first spoken: "Life is a marathon, not a sprint." That's why wise travelers (like you) select a traveling companion who never tires and never falters. That partner, of course, is your Heavenly Father.

The next time you find your courage tested by an unwelcome change, remember that God is as near as your next breath, and remember that He offers strength and comfort to His children. He is your shield and your strength; He is your protector and your deliverer. Call upon Him in your hour of need and then be comforted. Whatever your challenge, whatever your trouble, God can help you persevere. And that's precisely what He'll do if you ask Him.

Perhaps you are in a hurry for God to help you resolve your challenges. Perhaps you're anxious to earn the rewards that you feel you've already earned from life. Perhaps you're drumming your fingers, impatiently waiting for God to act. If so, be forewarned: God operates on His own timetable, not yours. Sometimes, God may answer your prayers with silence, and when He does, you must patiently persevere. In times of trouble, you must remain steadfast and trust in the merciful goodness of your Heavenly Father. Whatever your problem, He can handle it. Your job is to keep persevering until He does.

Look to Jesus

In a world filled with roadblocks and stumbling blocks, we need strength, courage, and perseverance. And, as an example of perfect perseverance, we need look no further than our Savior, Jesus Christ.

Jesus finished what He began. Despite the torture He endured, despite the shame of the cross, Jesus was steadfast in His faithfulness to God. We, too, must remain faithful, especially during times of hardship.

As you navigate the inevitable changes of modern-day life, you will undoubtedly experience your fair share of disappointments, detours, false starts, and failures. When you do, don't become discouraged: God's not finished with you yet.

More From God's Word About
Perseverance

Let us not become weary in doing good, for at the proper time we will reap a harvest if we do not give up.

Galatians 6:9 NIV

For you have need of endurance, so that when you have done the will of God, you may receive what was promised.

Hebrews 10:36 NASB

Thanks be to God! He gives us the victory through our Lord Jesus Christ. Therefore, my dear brothers, stand firm. Let nothing move you. Always give yourselves fully to the work of the Lord, because you know that your labor in the Lord is not in vain.

1 Corinthians 15:57-58 NIV

Be diligent that ye may be found of him in peace, without spot, and blameless.

2 Peter 3:14 KJV

It is better to finish something than to start it. It is better to be patient than to be proud.

Ecclesiastes 7:8 NCV

More Powerful Ideas About Perseverance

As we wait on God, He helps us use the winds of adversity to soar above our problems. As the Bible says, "Those who wait on the LORD . . . shall mount up with wings like eagles."

Billy Graham

You cannot persevere unless there is a trial in your life. There can be no victories without battles; there can be no peaks without valleys. If you want the blessing, you must be prepared to carry the burden and fight the battle. God has to balance privileges with responsibilities, blessings with burdens, or else you and I will become spoiled, pampered children.

Warren Wiersbe

The sermon of your life in tough times ministers to people more powerfully than the most eloquent speaker.

Bill Bright

Failure is one of life's most powerful teachers. How we handle our failures determines whether we're going to simply "get by" in life or "press on."

Beth Moore

Day 11

Take Comfort:
You Are Never Alone

The Lord is the One who will go before you. He will be with you; He will not leave you or forsake you. Do not be afraid or discouraged.

Deuteronomy 31:8 HCSB

If God is everywhere, why does He sometimes seem so far away? The answer to that question, of course, has nothing to do with God and everything to do with us.

When we begin each day on our knees, in praise and worship to Him, God often seems very near indeed. But, if we ignore God's presence or—worse yet—rebel against it altogether, the world in which we live becomes a spiritual wasteland.

Are you tired, discouraged, or fearful? Be comforted because God is with you. Are you confused? Listen to the quiet voice of your Heavenly Father. Are you bitter? Talk with God and seek His guidance. Are you celebrating a great victory? Thank God and praise Him. He is the Giver of all things good.

In whatever condition you find yourself, wherever you are, whether you are happy or sad, victorious or vanquished, troubled or triumphant, celebrate God's presence. And be comforted. God is not just near. He is here.

Quiet Moments with God

We live in an ever-changing, fast-paced world. The demands of everyday life can seem overwhelming at times, but when we slow ourselves down and seek the presence of a loving God, we invite His peace into our hearts.

Do you set aside quiet moments each day to offer praise to your Creator? You should. During these moments of stillness, you will often sense the infinite love and power of our Lord.

The familiar words of Psalm 46:10 remind us to "Be still, and know that I am God." When we do so, we encounter the awesome presence of our loving Heavenly Father, and we are comforted in the knowledge that God is not just near. He is here.

Get yourself into the presence of the loving
Father. Just place yourself before Him,
and look up into, His face; think of His love,
His wonderful, tender, pitying love.

—

Andrew Murray

More From God's Word About
God's Presence

Come near to God, and God will come near to you. You sinners, clean sin out of your lives. You who are trying to follow God and the world at the same time, make your thinking pure.

James 4:8 NCV

Again, this is God's command: to believe in his personally named Son, Jesus Christ. He told us to love each other, in line with the original command. As we keep his commands, we live deeply and surely in him, and he lives in us. And this is how we experience his deep and abiding presence in us: by the Spirit he gave us.

1 John 3:23-24 MSG

For the eyes of the Lord range throughout the earth to strengthen those whose hearts are fully committed to him.

2 Chronicles 16:9 NIV

God did this so that men would seek him and perhaps reach out for him and find him, though he is not far from each one of us.

Acts 17:27 NIV

More Powerful Ideas About
God's Presence

God's silence is in no way indicative of His activity or involvement in our lives. He may be silent, but He is not still.

Charles Swindoll

We should learn to live in the presence of the living God. He should be a well for us: delightful, comforting, unfailing, springing up to eternal life (John 4:14). When we rely on other people, their water supplies ultimately dry up. But, the well of the Creator never fails to nourish us.

C. H. Spurgeon

Certainly, God is with us in times of distress, and that is a comforting truth. But listen: Jesus wants to be part of every experience and every moment of our lives.

Billy Graham

God is in the midst of whatever has happened, is happening, and will happen.

Charles Swindoll

Day 12

Learn to Accept the Things You Cannot Change

For everything created by God is good, and nothing should be rejected if it is received with thanksgiving.

1 Timothy 4:4 HCSB

Are you embittered by an unexpected change or an unwelcome challenge that you did not deserve and cannot understand? If so, it's time to accept the unchangeable past and to have faith in the promise of tomorrow. It's time to trust God completely—and it's time to reclaim the peace—His peace—that can and should be yours.

On occasion, you will be confronted with situations that you simply don't understand. But God does. And He has a reason for everything that He does.

God doesn't explain Himself in ways that we, as mortals with limited insight and clouded vision, can comprehend. So, instead of understanding every aspect of God's unfolding plan for our lives and our universe, we must be satisfied to trust Him completely. We cannot know God's motivations, nor can we understand His actions. We can, however, trust Him, and we must.

When Dreams Don't Come True

Some of our most important dreams are the ones we abandon. Some of our most important goals are the ones we don't attain. Sometimes, our most important journeys are the ones that we take to the winding conclusion of what seem to be dead-end streets. Thankfully, with God there are no dead ends; there are only opportunities to learn, to yield, to trust, to serve, and to grow.

The next time you experience one of life's inevitable disappointments, don't despair and don't be afraid to try "Plan B." Consider every setback an opportunity to choose a different, more appropriate path. Have faith that God may indeed be leading you in an entirely different direction, a direction of His choosing. And as you take your next step, remember that what looks like a dead end to you may, in fact, be the fast lane according to God.

Have courage for the great sorrows of life
and patience for the small ones, and when you
have laboriously accomplished your daily task,
go to sleep in peace. God is awake.

—

Victor Hugo

More From God's Word About
Acceptance

A man's heart plans his way, but the Lord determines his steps.

Proverbs 16:9 HCSB

Do not remember the past events, pay no attention to things of old. Look, I am about to do something new; even now it is coming. Do you not see it? Indeed, I will make a way in the wilderness, rivers in the desert.

Isaiah 43:18-19 HCSB

Should we accept only good from God and not adversity?

Job 2:10 HCSB

Come to terms with God and be at peace; in this way good will come to you.

Job 22:21 HCSB

Sheathe your sword! Should I not drink the cup that the Father has given Me?

John 18:11 HCSB

More Powerful Ideas About
Acceptance

Surrender to the Lord is not a tremendous sacrifice, not an agonizing performance. It is the most sensible thing you can do.

Corrie ten Boom

He does not need to transplant us into a different field. He transforms the very things that were before our greatest hindrances, into the chief and most blessed means of our growth. No difficulties in your case can baffle Him. Put yourself absolutely into His hands, and let Him have His own way with you.

Elisabeth Elliot

In the kingdom of God, the surest way to lose something is to try to protect it, and the best way to keep it is to let it go.

A. W. Tozer

Acceptance is taking from God's hand absolutely anything He gives, looking into His face in trust and thanksgiving, knowing that the confinement of the situation we're in is good and for His glory.

Charles Swindoll

Day 13

Managing Stress

The peace of God, which surpasses all understanding,
will guard your hearts and minds through Christ Jesus.

Philippians 4:7 NKJV

Stressful days are an inevitable fact of modern life. And how do we best cope with the challenges of our demanding world? By turning our days and our lives over to God. Elisabeth Elliot writes, "If my life is surrendered to God, all is well. Let me not grab it back, as though it were in peril in His hand but would be safer in mine!" Yet even the most devout Christian woman may, at times, seek to grab the reins of her life and proclaim, "I'm in charge!" To do so is foolish, prideful, and stressful.

When we seek to impose our own will upon the world—or upon other people—we invite stress into our lives . . . needlessly. But, when we turn our lives and our hearts over to God—when we accept His will instead of seeking vainly to impose our own—we discover the inner peace that can be ours through Him.

Do you feel overwhelmed by the stresses of daily life? Turn your concerns and your prayers over to God. Trust Him. Trust Him completely. Trust Him today. Trust Him always. When it comes to the inevitable challenges of this day, hand them over to God completely and without reservation. He knows your needs and will meet those needs in His own way and in His own time if you let Him.

Slowing Down the Merry-go-round

Every major change, whether bad or good, puts stress on you and your family. That's why it's sensible to plan things so that you don't invite too many changes into your life at once. Of course: you'll be tempted to do otherwise. Once you land that new job, you'll be sorely tempted to buy the new house and the new car. Or if you've just gotten married, you'll be tempted to buy everything in sight—while the credit card payments mount. Don't do it!

When it comes to making big changes or big purchases, proceed slowly. Otherwise, you may find yourself uncomfortably perched atop a merry-go-round that is much easier to start than it is to stop.

> ### Stress is the intangible partner of progress.
> —
> *Charles Stanley*

More From God's Word About
Overcoming Adversity

LORD, help! they cried in their trouble, and he saved them from their distress.

Psalm 107:13 NLT

You have allowed me to suffer much hardship, but you will restore me to life again and lift me up from the depths of the earth. You will restore me to even greater honor and comfort me once again.

Psalm 71:20-21 NLT

When my heart is overwhelmed: lead me to the rock that is higher than I.

Psalm 61:2 KJV

God, who comforts the downcast, comforted us....

2 Corinthians 7:6 NIV

Trust God from the bottom of your heart; don't try to figure out everything on your own. Listen for God's voice in everything you do, everywhere you go; he's the one who will keep you on track.

Proverbs 3:5-6 MSG

More Powerful Ideas About Managing Stress

The better acquainted you become with God, the less tensions you feel and the more peace you possess.

Charles Allen

The happiest people I know are the ones who have learned how to hold everything loosely and have given the worrisome, stress-filled, fearful details of their lives into God's keeping.

Charles Swindoll

When frustrations develop into problems that stress you out, the best way to cope is to stop, catch your breath, and do something for yourself, not out of selfishness, but out of wisdom.

Barbara Johnson

Satan does some of his worst work on exhausted Christians when nerves are frayed and the mind is faint.

Vance Havner

Don't be overwhelmed. Take it one day and one prayer at a time.

Stormie Omartian

Day 14

Self-Esteem According
to God

For you made us only a little lower than God, and you crowned us with glory and honor.

Psalm 8:5 NLT

When you encounter tough times, you may lose self-confidence. Or you may become so focused on what other people are thinking—or saying—that you fail to focus on God. To do so is a mistake of major proportions—don't make it. Instead, seek God's guidance as you focus your energies on becoming the best you that you can possibly be. And when it comes to matters of self-esteem and self-image, seek approval not from your peers, but from your Creator.

Millions of words have been written about various ways to improve self-image and increase self-esteem. Yet, maintaining a healthy self-image is, to a surprising extent, a matter of doing three things: 1. Obeying God 2. Thinking healthy thoughts 3. Finding a purpose for your life that pleases your Creator and yourself. The following common-sense, Biblically-based tips can help you build the kind of self-image—and the kind of life—that both you and God can be proud of:

1. Do the right thing: If you're misbehaving, how can you possibly hope to feel good about yourself? (See Romans 14:12)

2. Watch what you think: If your inner voice is, in reality, your inner critic, you need to tone down the criticism now. And while you're at it, train yourself to begin thinking thoughts that are more rational, more accepting, and less judgmental. (Philippians 4:8)

3. Spend time with boosters, not critics: Are your friends putting you down? If so, find new friends. (Hebrews 3:13)

4. Don't be a perfectionist: Strive for excellence, but never confuse it with perfection. (Ecclesiastes 11:4, 6)

5. If you're addicted to something unhealthy, stop; if you can't stop, get help: Addictions, of whatever type, create havoc in your life. And disorder. And grief. And low self-esteem. (Exodus 20:3)

6. Find a purpose for your life that is larger than you are: When you're dedicated to something or someone besides yourself, you blossom. (Ephesians 6:7)

7. Don't worry too much about self-esteem: Instead, worry more about living a life that is pleasing to God. Learn to think optimistically. Find a worthy purpose. Find people to love and people to serve. When you do, your self-esteem will, on most days, take care of itself.

More From God's Word About Your Self-Worth

You're blessed when you're content with just who you are—no more, no less. That's the moment you find yourselves proud owners of everything that can't be bought.

Matthew 5:5 MSG

A devout life does bring wealth, but it's the rich simplicity of being yourself before God.

1 Timothy 6:6 MSG

You made all the delicate, inner parts of my body and knit me together in my mother's womb. Thank you for making me so wonderfully complex! Your workmanship is marvelous—and how well I know it.

Psalm 139:13-14 NLT

My dear children, let's not just talk about love; let's practice real love. This is the only way we'll know we're living truly, living in God's reality. It's also the way to shut down debilitating self-criticism, even when there is something to it. For God is greater than our worried hearts and knows more about us than we do ourselves. And friends, once that's taken care of and we're no longer accusing or condemning ourselves, we're bold and free before God!

1 John 3:18-21 MSG

More Powerful Ideas About
Your Self-Worth

As you and I lay up for ourselves living, lasting treasures in Heaven, we come to the awesome conclusion that we ourselves are His treasure!

Anne Graham Lotz

The Creator has made us each one of a kind. There is nobody else exactly like us, and there never will be. Each of us is his special creation and is alive for a distinctive purpose.

Luci Swindoll

Comparison is the root of all feelings of inferiority.

James Dobson

When it comes to our position before God, we're perfect. When he sees each of us, he sees one who has been made perfect through the One who is perfect—Jesus Christ.

Max Lucado

Give yourself a gift today: be present with yourself. God is. Enjoy your own personality. God does.

Barbara Johnson

Day 15

Consider the Possibilities

For nothing will be impossible with God.

Luke 1:37 HCSB

As you think about ways to manage change and embrace it, don't put limitations on God. He has the power to do miraculous things with you and through you . . . if you let Him.

Are you afraid to ask God to do big things—or to make big changes—in your life? Is your faith threadbare and worn? If so, it's time to abandon your doubts and reclaim your faith in God's promises.

Ours is a God of infinite possibilities. But sometimes, because of limited faith and limited understanding, we wrongly assume that God cannot or will not intervene in the affairs of mankind. Such assumptions are simply wrong.

God's Holy Word makes it clear: absolutely nothing is impossible for the Lord. And since the Bible means what it says, you can be comforted in the knowledge that the Creator of the universe can do miraculous things in your own life and in the lives of your loved ones. Your challenge, as a believer, is to take God at His word, and to expect the miraculous.

Opportunities Everywhere

As you look at the landscape of your life, do you see opportunities, possibilities, and blessings, or do you focus, instead, upon the more negative scenery? Do you spend more time counting your blessings or your misfortunes? If you've acquired the unfortunate habit of focusing too intently upon the negative aspects of life, then your spiritual vision is in need of correction.

Whether you realize it or not, opportunities are whirling around you like stars crossing the night sky: beautiful to observe, but too numerous to count. Yet you may be too concerned with the challenges of everyday living to notice those opportunities. That's why you should slow down occasionally, catch your breath, and focus your thoughts on two things: the talents God has given you and the opportunities that He has placed before you. God is leading you in the direction of those opportunities. Your task is to watch carefully, to pray fervently, and to act accordingly.

Man's adversity is God's opportunity.

—

Matthew Henry

More From God's Word
About Possibilities

Let us not lose heart in doing good, for in due time we shall reap if we do not grow weary. So then, while we have opportunity, let us do good to all men, and especially to those who are of the household of the faith.

Galatians 6:9-10 NASB

Make the most of every opportunity.

Colossians 4:5 NIV

God is our refuge and strength, a helper who is always found in times of trouble.

Psalm 46:1 HCSB

Dear brothers and sisters, whenever trouble comes your way, let it be an opportunity for joy. For when your faith is tested, your endurance has a chance to grow. So let it grow, for when your endurance is fully developed, you will be strong in character and ready for anything.

James 1:2-4 NLT

Remember ye not the former things, neither consider the things of old. Behold, I will do a new thing....

Isaiah 43:18-19 KJV

More Powerful Ideas About Possibilities

Often God shuts a door in our face so that he can open the door through which he wants us to go.

Catherine Marshall

Do we not continually pass by blessings innumerable without notice, and instead fix our eyes on what we feel to be our trials and our losses? And, do we not think and talk about our trials until our whole horizon is filled with them, and we almost begin to think we have no blessings at all?

Hannah Whitall Smith

Allow your dreams a place in your prayers and plans. God-given dreams can help you move into the future He is preparing for you.

Barbara Johnson

When God is involved, anything can happen. Be open and stay that way. God has a beautiful way of bringing good vibrations out of broken chords.

Charles Swindoll

God specializes in taking tragedy and turning it into triumph. The greater the tragedy, the greater the potential for triumph.

Charles Stanley

Day 16

Your Very Bright Future

For I know the thoughts that I think toward you, says the Lord, thoughts of peace and not of evil, to give you a future and a hope. Then you will call upon Me and go and pray to Me, and I will listen to you.

Jeremiah 29:11-12 NKJV

Because we are saved by a risen Christ, we can have hope for the future, no matter how troublesome our present circumstances may seem. After all, God has promised that we are His throughout eternity. And, He has told us that we must place our hopes in Him.

We will face disappointments and failures while we are here on earth, but these are only temporary defeats. This world can be a place of trials and tribulations, but when we place our trust in the Giver of all things good, we are secure. God has promised us peace, joy, and eternal life. And God keeps His promises today, tomorrow, and forever.

Are you willing to place your future in the hands of a loving and all-knowing God? Do you trust in the ultimate goodness of His plan for your life? Will you face today's challenges with optimism and hope? You should. After all, God created you for a very important purpose: His purpose. And you still have important work to do: His work.

Today, as you live in the present and look to the future, remember that God has a plan for you. Act—and believe—accordingly.

Our future may look fearfully intimidating, yet we can look up to the Engineer of the Universe, confident that nothing escapes His attention or slips out of the control of those strong hands.

—

Elisabeth Elliot

More From God's Word About
God's Guidance

In all your ways acknowledge Him, and He shall direct your paths.

Proverbs 3:6 NKJV

For now we see indistinctly, as in a mirror, but then face to face. Now I know in part, but then I will know fully, as I am fully known.

1 Corinthians 13:12 HCSB

However, each one must live his life in the situation the Lord assigned when God called him.

1 Corinthians 7:17 HCSB

The earth and everything in it, the world and its inhabitants, belong to the Lord.

Psalm 24:1 HCSB

My cup runs over. Surely goodness and mercy shall follow me all the days of my life; and I will dwell in the house of the Lord forever.

Psalm 23:5-6 NKJV

More Powerful Ideas About
Your Future

The future lies all before us. Shall it only be a slight advance upon what we usually do? Ought it not to be a bound, a leap forward to altitudes of endeavor and success undreamed of before?

Annie Armstrong

Every experience God gives us, every person he brings into our lives, is the perfect preparation for the future that only he can see.

Corrie ten Boom

The Christian believes in a fabulous future.

Billy Graham

Fix your eyes upon the Lord! Do it once. Do it daily. Do it constantly. Look at the Lord and keep looking at Him.

Charles Swindoll

God's plan for our guidance is for us to grow gradually in wisdom before we get to the crossroads.

Bill Hybels

Day 17

Live Courageously

They do not fear bad news; they confidently trust the Lord to care for them. They are confident and fearless and can face their foes triumphantly.

Psalm 112:7-8 NLT

Every person's life is a tapestry of events: some wonderful, some not-so-wonderful, and some downright disastrous. When we visit the mountaintops of life, praising God isn't hard—in fact, it's easy. In our moments of triumph, we can bow our heads and thank God for our victories. But when we fail to reach the mountaintops, we find it much tougher to give God the praise He deserves. Yet wherever we find ourselves, whether on the mountaintops of life or in life's darkest valleys, we must still offer thanks to God, giving thanks in all circumstances.

The next time you find yourself worried about the challenges of today or the uncertainties of tomorrow, ask yourself this question: are you really ready to place your concerns and your life in God's all-powerful, all-knowing, all-loving hands? If the answer to that question is yes—as it should be—then you can draw courage today from the source of strength that never fails: your Father in heaven.

God is not a distant being. He is not absent from our world, nor is He absent from your world. God is not "out there"; He is "right here," continuously reshaping His universe, and continuously reshaping the lives of those who dwell in it.

God is with you always, listening to your thoughts and prayers, watching over your every move. If the demands of everyday life weigh down upon you, you may be tempted to ignore God's presence or—worse yet—to lose faith in His promises. But, when you quiet yourself and acknowledge His presence, God will touch your heart and restore your courage.

At this very moment—as you're fulfilling your obligations and overcoming tough times—God is seeking to work in you and through you. He's asking you to live abundantly and courageously . . . and He's ready to help.

Faith not only can help you through a crisis,
it can help you to approach life after the hard
times with a whole new perspective. It can help
you adopt an outlook of hope and courage
through faith to face reality.

—

John Maxwell

More From God's Word About Courage

Be strong and courageous, and do the work. Don't be afraid or discouraged by the size of the task, for the LORD God, my God, is with you. He will not fail you or forsake you.

1 Chronicles 28:20 NLT

Therefore, being always of good courage . . . we walk by faith, not by sight.

2 Corinthians 5:6-7 NASB

God doesn't want us to be shy with his gifts, but bold and loving and sensible.

2 Timothy 1:7 MSG

The LORD himself goes before you and will be with you; he will never leave you nor forsake you. Do not be afraid; do not be discouraged.

Deuteronomy 31:8 NIV

But Moses said to the people, "Do not fear! Stand by and see the salvation of the LORD."

Exodus 14:13 NASB

More Powerful Ideas About Courage

Seeing that a Pilot steers the ship in which we sail, who will never allow us to perish even in the midst of shipwrecks, there is no reason why our minds should be overwhelmed with fear and overcome with weariness.

John Calvin

Like dynamite, God's power is only latent power until it is released. You can release God's dynamite power into people's lives and into the world through faith, through words, and through prayer.

Bill Bright

Faith is stronger than fear.

John Maxwell

Do not let Satan deceive you into being afraid of God's plans for your life.

R. A. Torrey

Jesus Christ can make the weakest man into a divine dreadnought, fearing nothing.

Oswald Chambers

Day 18

Ask Him

So I say to you, keep asking, and it will be given to you. Keep searching, and you will find. Keep knocking, and the door will be opened to you.

Luke 11:9 HCSB

How often do you ask God for His help and His wisdom? Occasionally? Intermittently? Whenever you experience a crisis? Hopefully not. Hopefully, you've acquired the habit of asking for God's assistance early and often. And if you've acquired that habit, it will serve you well, especially when you experience the pangs of grief.

Jesus made it clear to His disciples: they should petition God to meet their needs. So should you. Genuine, heartfelt prayer has the potential to produce powerful changes in you and in your world.

God can help you begin the process of moving through and beyond your grief. He can dry your tears and calm your fears if you have the courage to ask Him (and the determination to keep asking Him). But when it comes to grief work (or any other kind of work, for that matter), please don't expect God to do it all; He intends for you to help. When you do your part, He will do His part—and when He does, you can expect miraculous results.

The Bible promises that God will guide you if you let Him. Your job is to let Him. God has promised that when you ask for His help, He will not withhold it. So ask. Ask Him to meet your needs moment by moment, day by day, week by week, and year by year. Ask Him to lead you, to protect you, to correct you, and to heal you.

God stands at the door and waits. When you knock, He opens. When you ask, He answers. Your task, of course, is to make God a full partner in every aspect of your life—in good times and hard times—and to seek His guidance prayerfully, confidently, and often.

Don't be afraid to ask your
Heavenly Father for anything you need.
Indeed, nothing is too small for
God's attention or too great
for his power.

—

Dennis Swanberg

More From God's Word About
Asking God

Do not worry about anything, but pray and ask God for everything you need, always giving thanks.

Philippians 4:6 NCV

You do not have, because you do not ask God.

James 4:2 NIV

Verily, verily, I say unto you, He that believeth on me, the works that I do shall he do also; and greater works than these shall he do; because I go unto my Father. And whatsoever ye shall ask in my name, that will I do, that the Father may be glorified in the Son. If ye shall ask any thing in my name, I will do it.

John 14:12-14 KJV

You did not choose me, but I chose you and appointed you to go and bear fruit—fruit that will last. Then the Father will give you whatever you ask in my name.

John 15:16 NIV

If you need wisdom—if you want to know what God wants you to do—ask him, and he will gladly tell you. He will not resent your asking.

James 1:5 NLT

More Powerful Ideas About
Asking God

The God of the galaxies is the God who knows when your heart is broken—and He can heal it!

Warren Wiersbe

You don't have to be alone in your hurt! Comfort is yours. Joy is an option. And it's all been made possible by your Savior. He went without comfort so you might have it. He postponed joy so you might share in it. He willingly chose isolation so you might never be alone in your hurt and sorrow.

Joni Eareckson Tada

When you ask God to do something, don't ask timidly; put your whole heart into it.

Marie T. Freeman

God will help us become the people we are meant to be, if only we will ask Him.

Hannah Whitall Smith

Some people think God does not like to be troubled with our constant asking. But, the way to trouble God is not to come at all.

D. L. Moody

Day 19

God Does Not Change

Be still, and know that I am God.

Psalm 46:10 NKJV

These are times of great uncertainty. As we become accustomed to, and at times almost numbed by, a steady stream of unsettling news, we are reminded that our world is in a state of constant change. But God is not. So when the world seems to be trembling beneath our feet, we can be comforted in the knowledge that our Heavenly Father is the rock that cannot be shaken. His Word promises, "I am the Lord, I do not change" (Malachi 3:6 NKJV).

Every day that we live, we mortals encounter a multitude of changes—some good, some not so good. And on occasion, all of us must endure life-changing personal losses that leave us heartbroken. When we do, our Heavenly Father stands ready to comfort us, to guide us, and—in time—to heal us.

Is the world spinning a little too fast for your liking? Are you facing troubling uncertainties, difficult circumstances, or unwelcome changes? If so, please remember that God is far bigger than any problem you may face. So, instead of worrying about life's inevitable challenges, put your faith in the Father and His only begotten Son. After all, "Jesus Christ is the same yesterday, today, and forever" (Hebrews 13:8 NKJV). And it is precisely because your Savior does not change that you can face your challenges with courage for today and hope for tomorrow.

Are you anxious about situations that you cannot control? Take your anxieties to God. Are you troubled? Take your troubles to Him. Does your little corner of the universe seem to be a frightening place? Seek protection from the One who cannot be moved. The same God who created the universe will protect you if you ask Him . . . .so ask Him . . . and then serve Him with willing hands and a trusting heart.

Number one, God brought me here.
It is by His will that I am in this place. In that fact I will rest. Number two, He will keep me here in His love and give me grace to behave as His child. Number three, He will make the trial a blessing, teaching me the lessons He intends for me to learn and working in me the grace He means to bestow. Number four, in His good time He can bring me out again. How and when, He knows. So, let me say I am here.

—

Andrew Murray

More From God's Word About
God's Love

We know how much God loves us, and we have put our trust in him. God is love, and all who live in love live in God, and God lives in them.

1 John 4:16 NLT

As the Father loved Me, I also have loved you; abide in My love.

John 15:9 NKJV

The unfailing love of the LORD never ends! By his mercies we have been kept from complete destruction.

Lamentations 3:22 NLT

Whoever is wise will observe these things, and they will understand the lovingkindness of the Lord.

Psalm 107:43 NKJV

For God loved the world in this way: He gave His only Son, so that everyone who believes in Him will not perish but have eternal life.

John 3:16 HCSB

More Powerful Ideas About God's Protection

Sometimes we need a birds-eye view of what God sees about our lives. If we could just see what he sees we might lighten up a little bit.

Dennis Swanberg

Under heaven's lock and key, we are protected by the most efficient security system available: the power of God.

Charles Swindoll

In all the old castles of England, there was a place called the keep. It was always the strongest and best protected place in the castle, and in it were hidden all who were weak and helpless and unable to defend themselves in times of danger. Shall we be afraid to hide ourselves in the keeping power of our Divine Keeper, who neither slumbers nor sleeps, and who has promised to preserve our going out and our coming in, from this time forth and even forever more?

Hannah Whitall Smith

He is within and without. His Spirit dwells within me. His armor protects me. He goes before me and is behind me.

Mary Morrison Suggs

Day 20

The Power of Hope

I wait for the Lord; I wait, and put my hope in His word.

Psalm 130:5 HCSB

There are few sadder sights on earth than the sight of a man or woman who has lost all hope. In difficult times, hope can be elusive, but those who place their faith in God's promises need never lose it. After all, God is good; His love endures; He has promised His children the gift of eternal life. And, God keeps His promises.

Despite God's promises, despite Christ's love, and despite our countless blessings, we frail human beings can still lose hope from time to time. When we do, we need the encouragement of trusted friends, the life-changing power of prayer, and the healing truth of God's Holy Word.

If you find yourself falling into the spiritual traps of worry and discouragement, seek the healing touch of Jesus and the encouraging words of fellow Christians. If you find a friend in need, remind him or her of the peace that is found through a personal relationship with Christ. It was Christ who promised, "These things I have spoken unto you, that in me ye might have peace. In the world ye shall have tribulation: but be of good cheer; I have overcome the world" (John 16:33 KJV). This world can be a place of trials and tribulations, but as believers, we are secure. God has promised us peace, joy, and eternal life. And, of course, God keeps His promises today, tomorrow, and forever.

People are genuinely motivated
by hope and a part of that hope is
the assurance of future glory with God
for those who are His people.

—

Warren Wiersbe

More From God's Word About Hope

Let us hold on to the confession of our hope without
wavering, for He who promised is faithful.

Hebrews 10:23 HCSB

Hope deferred makes the heart sick.

Proverbs 13:12 NKJV

Sustain me as You promised, and I will live; do not let
me be ashamed of my hope.

Psalm 119:116 HCSB

For I know the thoughts that I think toward you, says
the Lord, thoughts of peace and not of evil, to give you
a future and a hope. Then you will call upon Me and go
and pray to Me, and I will listen to you.

Jeremiah 29:11-12 NKJV

Be of good courage, and He shall strengthen your heart,
all you who hope in the Lord.

Psalm 31:24 NKJV

More Powerful Ideas About Hope

I wish I could make it all new again; I can't. But God can. "He restores my soul," wrote the shepherd. God doesn't reform; he restores. He doesn't camouflage the old; he restores the new. The Master Builder will pull out the original plan and restore it. He will restore the vigor, he will restore the energy. He will restore the hope. He will restore the soul.

Max Lucado

Faith looks back and draws courage; hope looks ahead and keeps desire alive.

John Eldredge

I discovered that sorrow was not to be feared but rather endured with hope and expectancy that God would use it to visit and bless my life.

Jill Briscoe

Oh, remember this: There is never a time when we may not hope in God. Whatever our necessities, however great our difficulties, and though to all appearance help is impossible, yet our business is to hope in God; and it will be found that it is not in vain.

George Mueller

Day 21

The Ultimate Comfort,
the Ultimate Protection

The Lord is my rock, my fortress, and my deliverer.

Psalm 18:2 HCSB

The hand of God encircles us and comforts us in times of adversity. In times of hardship, He restores our strength; in times of sorrow, He dries our tears. When we are troubled, or weak, or embittered, God is as near as our next breath.

God has promised to protect us, and He intends to fulfill His promise. In a world filled with dangers and temptations, God is the ultimate armor. In a world filled with misleading messages, God's Word is the ultimate truth. In a world filled with more frustrations than we can count, God's Son offers the ultimate peace.

Will you accept God's peace and wear God's armor against the dangers of our world? Hopefully so, because when you do, you can live courageously, knowing that you possess the ultimate protection: God's unfailing love for you.

You Are Protected

Although God has probably guided you through many struggles and more than a few difficult days, you may still find your faith stretched to the limit whenever you encounter adversity, uncertainty, or unwelcome changes. But the good news is this: Even though your circumstances may change, God's love for you does not.

The next time you find yourself facing a fear-provoking situation, remember that no challenge is too big for your Heavenly Father, not even yours. And while you're thinking about the scope of God's power and His love, ask yourself which is stronger: your faith or your fear. The answer should be obvious.

Wherever you are, God is there, too. And, because He cares for you today and always, you are protected.

Being loved by Him whose opinion matters most gives us the security to risk loving, too—even loving ourselves.

—

Gloria Gaither

More From God's Word About
God's Protection

The Lord bless you and protect you; the Lord make His face shine on you, and be gracious to you.

Numbers 6:24-25 HCSB

The Lord your God in your midst, The Mighty One, will save; He will rejoice over you with gladness, He will quiet you with His love, He will rejoice over you with singing.

Zephaniah 3:17 NKJV

God is my shield, saving those whose hearts are true and right.

Psalm 7:10 NLT

Those who trust the Lord are like Mount Zion, which sits unmoved forever. As the mountains surround Jerusalem, the Lord surrounds his people now and forever.

Psalm 125:1-2 NCV

Finally, my brethren, be strong in the Lord and in the power of His might. Put on the whole armor of God, that you may be able to stand against the wiles of the devil.

Ephesians 6:10-11 NKJV

More Powerful Ideas About
God's Protection

The Rock of Ages is the great sheltering encirclement.

Oswald Chambers

Under heaven's lock and key, we are protected by the most efficient security system available: the power of God.

Charles Swindoll

In all the old castles of England, there was a place called the keep. It was always the strongest and best protected place in the castle, and in it were hidden all who were weak and helpless and unable to defend themselves in times of danger. Shall we be afraid to hide ourselves in the keeping power of our Divine Keeper, who neither slumbers nor sleeps, and who has promised to preserve our going out and our coming in, from this time forth and even forever more?

Hannah Whitall Smith

There is not only fear, but terrible danger, for the life unguarded by God.

Oswald Chambers

Day 22

Follow Him

Then Jesus said to His disciples, "If anyone wants to come with Me, he must deny himself, take up his cross, and follow Me. For whoever wants to save his life will lose it, but whoever loses his life because of Me will find it."

Matthew 16:24-25 HCSB

Jesus walks with you. Are you walking with Him seven days a week, and not just on Sunday mornings? Are you a seven-day-a-week Christian who carries your faith with you to work each day, or do you try to keep Jesus at a "safe" distance when you're not sitting in church? Hopefully, you understand the wisdom of walking with Christ all day every day.

Jesus loved you so much that He endured unspeakable humiliation and suffering for you. How will you respond to Christ's sacrifice? Will you take up His cross and follow Him—during good times and tough times—or will you choose another path? When you place your hopes squarely at the foot of the cross, when you place Jesus squarely at the center of your life, you will be blessed.

Do you seek to fulfill God's purpose for your life? Do you seek spiritual abundance? Would you like to partake in "the peace that passes all understanding"? Then follow Christ. Follow Him by picking up His cross today and every day that you live. When you do, you will quickly discover that Christ's love has the power to change everything, including you.

Your Eternal Journey

Eternal life is not an event that begins when you die. Eternal life begins when you invite Jesus into your heart right here on earth. So it's important to remember that God's plans for you are not limited to the ups and downs of everyday life. If you've allowed Jesus to reign over your heart, you've already begun your eternal journey.

Today, give praise to the Creator for His priceless gift, the gift of eternal life. And then, when you've offered Him your thanks and your praise, share His Good News with all who cross your path.

You who suffer take heart.
Christis the answer to sorrow.

—

Billy Graham

More From God's Word About
Following Christ

Then he told them what they could expect for themselves: "Anyone who intends to come with me has to let me lead."

Luke 9:23 MSG

I've laid down a pattern for you. What I've done, you do.

John 13:15 MSG

No one can serve two masters. Either he will hate the one and love the other, or he will be devoted to the one and despise the other.

Matthew 6:24 NIV

Whoever is not willing to carry the cross and follow me is not worthy of me. Those who try to hold on to their lives will give up true life. Those who give up their lives for me will hold on to true life.

Matthew 10:38-39 NCV

If anyone would come after me, he must deny himself and take up his cross and follow me.

Mark 8:34 NIV

More Powerful Ideas About
Following Christ

Jesus Christ is not a security from storms. He is perfect security in storms.

Kathy Troccoli

In the midst of the pressure and the heat, I am confident His hand is on my life, developing my faith until I display His glory, transforming me into a vessel of honor that pleases Him!

Anne Graham Lotz

Sometimes we get tired of the burdens of life, but we know that Jesus Christ will meet us at the end of life's journey. And, that makes all the difference.

Billy Graham

The Lord gets His best soldiers out of the highlands of affliction.

C. H. Spurgeon

God takes us through struggles and difficulties so that we might become increasingly committed to Him.

Charles Swindoll